How They Change

by Joyce Markovics

Consultant: Kimberly Brenneman, PhD
National Institute for Early Education Research
Rutgers University
New Brunswick, New Jersey

New York, New York

Credits

TOC, © Shutterstock; 4–5, © Shutterstock; 6–7, © iStockphoto/Thinkstock; 8, © iStockphoto/Thinkstock; 9, © Shutterstock; 10–11, © Shutterstock; 12–13, © iStockphoto/Thinkstock; 14–15, © Rita Kochmarjova/Shutterstock; 16, © Eric Isselee/Shutterstock; 17, © Shutterstock; 18–19, © Shutterstock; 20–21, © Inhabitant/Shutterstock; 22, © Shutterstock; 23TL, © Shutterstock; 23TM, © Shutterstock; 23TR, © iStockphoto/Thinkstock; 23BL, © iStockphoto/Thinkstock; 23BM, © Shutterstock; 23BR, © iStockphoto/Thinkstock; 24, © Shutterstock.

Publisher: Kenn Goin
Senior Editor: Joyce Tavolacci
Creative Director: Spencer Brinker
Design: Debrah Kaiser
Photo Researcher: Michael Win

Library of Congress Cataloging-in-Publication Data

Markovics, Joyce L., author.
The seasons' colors : how they change / by Joyce Markovics.
pages cm. (Colors tell a story)
Includes bibliographical references and index.
ISBN 978-1-62724-327-8 (library binding) ISBN 1-62724-327-5 (library binding)
1. Seasons Juvenile literature. 2. Colors Juvenile literature. I. Title.
QC495.5.M368 2015
508.2 dc23
2014004637

For more information, write to Bearport Publishing Company, Inc., 45 West 21st Street, Suite 3B, New York, New York 10010. Printed in the United States of America.

10 9 8 7 6 5 4 3 2 1

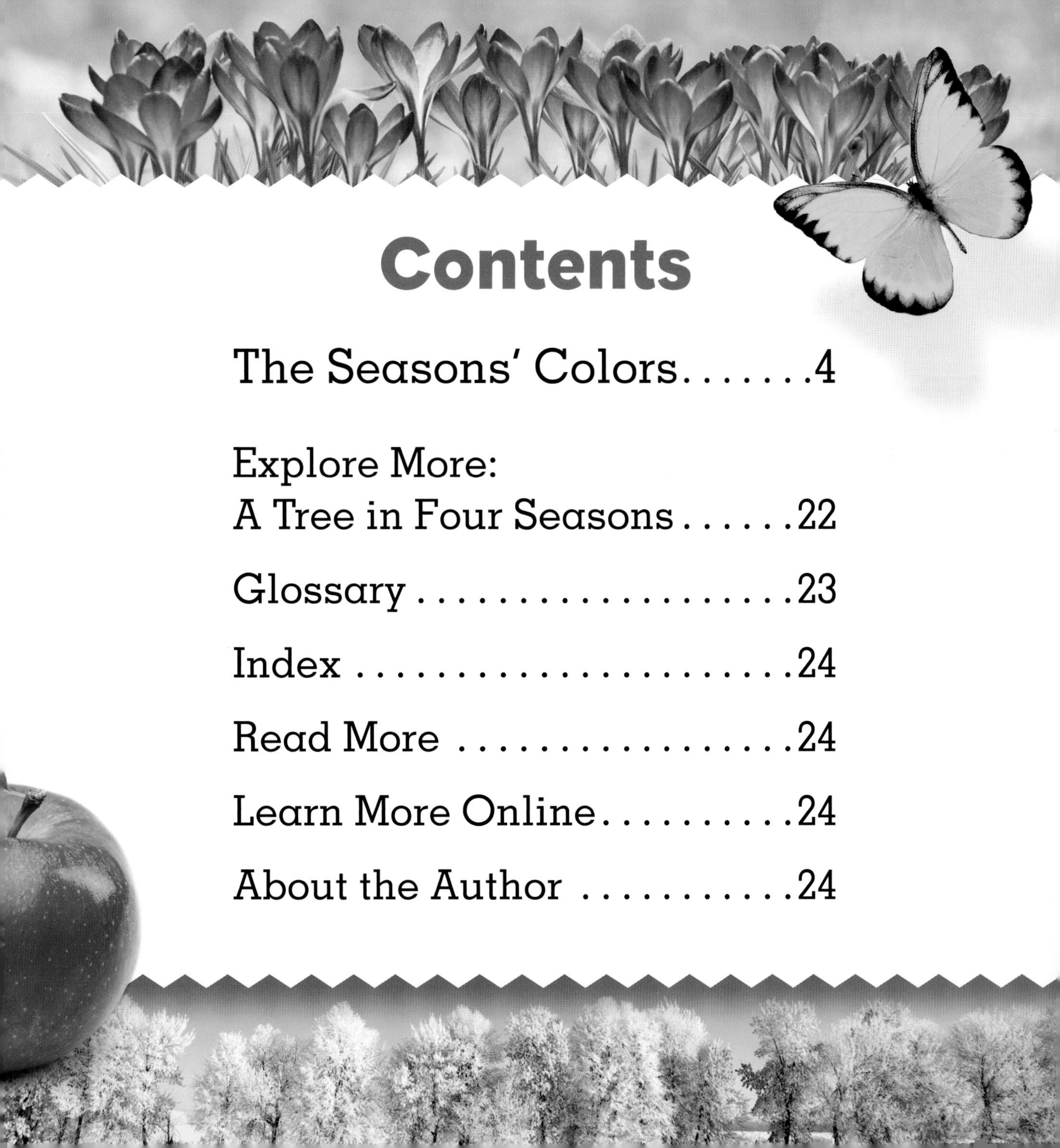

Contents

The Seasons' Colors 4

Explore More:
A Tree in Four Seasons 22

Glossary 23

Index 24

Read More 24

Learn More Online 24

About the Author 24

The Seasons' Colors

Colors tell a story about each season.

Let's see how nature's colors change in spring, summer, fall, and winter.

Spring

In spring, rain soaks into the ground.

The sun warms the air.

Then green **shoots** poke out of the soil.

Tiny pale-green leaves grow on branches.

Pink **buds** and blossoms cover trees.

Spring colors are all around.

Summer

As spring becomes summer, more colors appear.

Red flowers fill a garden.

A blue butterfly visits the **blooms**.

In summer, the sun shines.

Light-green leaves turn a darker shade.

They cover a forest in an **emerald** blanket.

Fall

To welcome fall, the leaves change once again.

They become yellow, red, and orange.

The leaves swirl
all around.

In fall, pumpkins **ripen** to a bright orange.

Then they are carved for Halloween.

Winter

Soon, days become shorter.

A chilly wind blows.

Winter arrives with **flurries** of white snow.

Tiny flakes cover a frozen pond until it's winter white.

In a few months, bits of green will tell that spring has come once again.

Explore More: A Tree in Four Seasons

You Will Need:

- A large piece of paper
- Markers
- A pair of scissors
- Colored paper
- Glue

As the seasons change, so do the colors of some trees. Explore the different colors of the seasons by making your own tree and showing how its colors change throughout the year.

How to Make Your Tree:

1. Divide a large piece of paper into four sections. Use a marker to draw the trunk and branches of a tree in each section.
2. Label each of the four sections: Spring; Summer; Fall; Winter.
3. Then decorate each tree to match the season. Use scissors to cut out bits of colored paper. Glue them on the branches.
4. When you are finished, show your poster to friends and family. Point out the different colors and explain how they change as the seasons do.

Glossary

blooms (BLOOMZ)
flowers

buds (BUHDZ) small growths on the stems of trees and other plants that turn into leaves or flowers

emerald (EM-ur-uhld)
a bright green color

flurries (FLUR-eez)
when snow lightly falls

ripen (RIPE-uhn)
to become ready to pick and eat

shoots (SHOOTS)
the new parts of a plant that are just starting to grow

Index

fall 5, 14–15, 16–17
spring 5, 6–7, 8–9
summer 5, 10–11, 12–13
winter 5, 18–19, 20–21

Read More

Eckart, Edana. *Watching the Seasons (Welcome Books).* New York: Children's Press (2004).

Esbaum, Jill. *Winter Wonderland.* Washington, D.C.: National Geographic (2010).

Learn More Online

To learn more about the seasons' colors, visit
www.bearportpublishing.com/ColorsTellaStory

About the Author

Joyce Markovics and her husband, Adam, live along the Hudson River in Tarrytown, New York, where the various colors of the seasons are always on spectacular display.